Hi, I'm Jenn Webster, a visionary spirit who always felt the profound calling to pen down all that ignites in my heart. Having an innate ability to resonate with and relate to others, my journey is not just mine. It's ours, intertwined by the shared experiences and common emotions that link us all together. On the path of relentless growth and self-discovery, I believe in evolving together, nourishing each other with grace, compassion, and endless inspiration. Join me in this beautiful journey where together, we flourish and foster a nurturing environment for growth.

Every day is a new opportunity for me to grow in grace, expanding my horizons, exploring my potential while inviting you to embark on this enlightening journey alongside me. Join me as we evolve, bloom, and find grace in each shared story and experienced moments. Together, let's inspire one another and let kindness and love leave footprints on our paths.

Welcome to the inspiring journey of a soul, led by purpose and faith, sharing the boundless love of Jesus Christ. As we grow in grace together, my writings aim to touch hearts and foster kinship. Not just an author, but also a dedicated wife and mom, my experiences intimately resonate with my readers, offering empathy and enlightenment. Join me as we navigate through life's beautiful challenges, hand in hand, heart to heart.

Lord, as we begin to take a deeper journey into the importance of getting silent, I ask that you touch each person taking the time to read this and grow closer to you. I ask that you show each one of us ways to accomplish this much needed silence and time with you. I thank you in advance for the opportunity to share my stories, my testimonies and mostly; the opportunity to share from a real perspective as we grow together. Lord, I thank you that this will be more than words on a page but that each person reading will feel connected and relatable to the journey and that they will experience your peace. *In Jesus name, Amen*

"We need to find God and He cannot be found in noise and restlessness. God is the friend of silence. See how nature – trees, flowers, grass – grows in silence; see the starts, the moon, the sun, how they move in silence... the more we receive in our silent prayer the more we can give in our active life.

We need silence to be able to touch souls. The

essential thing is not what we say, but what God

says to us and through us. All our words will be

useless unless they come from within- words

which do not give the light of Christ, increase

darkness." - Mother Theresa -

I have been inspired by Mother Theresa since I was probably eight years old. I always thought deeply about the things she said, and this is one of those quotes that stuck with me for a long time.

As I grew older and got lost in my own world and the things that had happened to me as a child, I forgot many of the things that I had once held dear to my heart. I forgot how to be in the silence.

When I prayed, I expected an answer immediately and, in a form, I could physically see, touch or hear. I stopped taking time to just, be.

God tells us in Psalm 46:10 "Be still and know that I am God".

Often, I think we forget that He is in fact, God and we are not. Not that we believe we are God in sense of having all his powers, abilities and knowing; but in the sense that we constantly try to figure everything out on our own without ever getting to the still, silent place to hear from Him.

We want God to move in ways that we do not necessarily allow Him to move in. We have this preconceived notion in our minds already of what the move of God should look like. I am willing to take a bet and say that most of the time the expectation of God's move is something big.

Mostly due to our wanting the immediate and usually, life changing result from Him.

When we look more into the idea of the word move or movement, in the Hebrew language the meaning is "to flutter". This put a different perspective on things for me. I began to think about how butterflies move so gently and softly. I thought about the first time I felt a baby move in the womb. When I thought of this word, flutter, all that came to mind was gentleness. I was reminded of how the birds gently move across the water and taken back to a night when God showed me how beautiful this really is.

It was early evening hours but being January, it was already dark outside. All I had to guide my walk were headlights from the passing cars and the few streetlights that were in working order.

I remember being in such a weird place of faith because I was struggling with the balance of being a single mom, working, making it to all of events my children had going on at school, paying all the bills on time, etc. A common struggle through society today, and not just in the life of a single parent anymore.

I was walking across a bridge over the lake, and I just took a moment to stop and take in the beauty that was there. The water was like a sheet of glass – not a wave or ripple to be seen. The streetlights reflected in just the right areas to be able to see the reflection of nearby trees and surrounding stones.

There was stillness in the atmosphere. I did not notice the passing cars. I completely forgot about what I was worrying about and just felt this peace come over me. Just as I was kind of settling into this peace a small flock of birds came across the lake, swooping down just enough to touch the edge of their wings in the water – giving off the most gentle fluttering sound as they moved the water.

I was taken to Genesis 1:2

And the earth was without form and void and darkness was upon the face of the deep. And the Spirit of God moved upon the face of the waters.

How often do we feel void, dark and maybe without form (purpose)? Is there something in your life right now that has you feeling dark, void or without form (purpose)? Write it down.

_____

_____

_____

_____

_____

Is there something you are waiting on God for, but struggling to get into that silence to have an intimate conversation with him about?

_____

_____

_____

_____

_____

_____

_____

_____

I don't know about you, but I have struggled with being able to get into that silent place. When it gets "quiet" I realize how much noise my refrigerator makes. I suddenly remember every single thing I forgot to do since the beginning of time. I realize that I need coffee creamer or begin to think about what I am going to make for dinner.

Then there are times when I seem to just start getting into that still, peaceful place and BAM one of my kids will knock on the door, someone starts crying, the mail carrier needs a signature on something. You know, any little distraction.

Sometimes, it feels like trying to get into the silent place with God is noisier than any other time of the day. I have found that there is a process for me to get there. For me, this process begins with music.

I am a firm believer that music can either prepare your heart and settle your mind or it can feed your mind and close your heart. What we listen to is very important.

Take a moment and consider 3 things you can do to help get into that silent place with God.

1)_____

_____

2)_____

_____

3)_____

_____

When we go back and look at that word, move or flutter, it means to persuade to prevail on, to excite from a state of rest or indifference.

I want to focus on the first part; to persuade to prevail on. Have you ever had to persuade someone to do something? What did that look like?

_____

_____

_____

_____

_____

_____

_____

_____

I heard a pastor say one time, "Your prayer is not the first time God found out about the situation. It is the first time you included him". I was thinking about this as I thought about the question myself. I thought, how many times have I tried to persuade God to do something?

When I began to look into what persuade means I noticed that it generally means to cause someone to do something by reasoning or argument.

Have you found yourself trying to persuade God? Trying to get him to answer your prayer according to how you want to see it answered opposed to trusting that His answer is going to be best – even if it does not look anything like what you think it should?

Abraham and Sarah are good examples of this.

God gave Abraham a promise and he trusted God. But ... there was a time... we know the story. Which I am putting into my own words here, but we know that they got impatient.

Sarah, looking at the circumstances, decided there must be something else that needs to be done for this promise from God to be fulfilled. She was probably battling with that void and without purpose feeling. So, she decided to take matters into her own hands and persuaded her husband to do something about it.

Now, I don't know about you, but I cannot relate to Sarah on this one. I cannot see myself convincing my husband to go ahead and have a baby with someone else. I know me enough to know I would be standing on that promise from God, even if I were struggling to fully believe it, I would totally use it before I let my husband be with another woman. We know how that story continues.

God still followed through on his promise! Even when they took matters into their own hands. So often though, don't we do the same thing? The fulfillment of a promise from God, or an answer to our prayer seems to be on hold for some reason; so, we take matters into our own hands.

Too often we try to reason things out by the standards of the world instead of by the standards of God. Why? Because it is easier to understand and process logically (most of the time anyway). God's ways are sometimes, ok, a lot of times, very difficult for us to comprehend but that is why it is so important to get into that silence with Him.

We start to look at our bank accounts, our age, our flaws, our failures, what we believe others expect from us... this list could go on and on about all the things we begin to look for to not only excuse what we are getting ready to do, but also what we have already done.

The point is this: we sometimes spend more time looking at what is missing or become so focused on what we want that we stop appreciating what we've got. We lose complacency and stop trusting God to do what God said He would do.

The flip side of this is that other times we become so dependent on God that we forget there are things we have to do as well. We end up working against God instead of with God.

Is there something you have been praying for or that you know God has given you a promise on – that you decided to move on before God's time?

_____

_____

_____

_____

_____

_____

_____

_____

How did it work out?

_____

_____

_____

_____

_____

_____

_____

_____

The Lord will fight for you, and you have only to be silent. Exodus 14:14

What are you trusting, praying or believing in the Lord for today?

Even Jesus needed time to get away from the noise of the world.

He would withdraw to desolate places and pray. Luke 5:16

How do you prepare your heart and mind to be

silent with the Lord?

_____

_____

_____

_____

_____

_____

_____

_____

I know you're probably thinking that we have already talked about this. When I asked you to write down 3 things you can do to help get into that silent place with God, but I'm asking you to go a little deeper this time. You may even go back and change or add to your answers in a few minutes, but I want you to take a moment to consider the condition of your heart when you are trying to get to that quiet space with God.

Do you wait until you are feeling completely stressed out?

Do you go into it with an agenda that is focused on yourself? Or even your friends or family?

Do you use it as time away or alone time instead

of truly trying to get into the presence of God?

Do you walk into that room, closet, basement, etc.

with your list of things you want to pray for and

focus on just that list?

Do you ... take time ... to just worship God; to thank Him for all that you have?

Have you taken time to prepare your heart to be open to whatever God has for you during that time?

I know I have found myself doing all of those things at one time or another. I found myself so lost at one point in everything going on around me; I went to my prayer space feeling completely angry. I was so mad about things that were going on around me, I was mad that I felt like God was ignoring me, I was mad that my son was sick all the time and the doctors refused to look into things more because his bloodwork looked fine. I was angry that my oldest son was struggling with following rules and finding himself in tons of trouble everywhere he turned. I was mad that I had made some of the choices that I had which led me to parts of my situation, but I couldn't undo them. I was just mad about everything.

So, when I walked into my prayer space; I did not go there with a heart ready to receive, I went there with a heart that literally just felt empty and a mind full of all the things I was mad about. I did not go to that prayer place truly seeking intimacy with God ... I wanted answers, I wanted my children to be healed, I wanted my situation to be changed; yet I went into this place – that was supposed to be silent and intimate with God and I heard nothing.

For months, I heard nothing ... nothing I wanted to hear anyway.

Isn't that what we do? So many times, we will go to God, but He doesn't tell us what we want to hear so we claim He isn't answering us or that we aren't hearing from him.

I think about Jesus and all the times he went to just spend time with God to be intimate with Him. Jesus knew what His purpose here on Earth was for and yet, even when He was worried; even when He was asking God –

He went a little farther and fell on His face, and prayed, saying, "O My Father, if it is possible, let this cup pass from Me; nevertheless, not as I will, but as You will." Matthew 26:39

Jesus did something so important here though; that we miss so many times. He did not want to do what He knew He had to do, even asked if there was any other way to make things happen. I imagine Jesus crying out to God ... please please don't make me do this.

How many times do we cry out to God, sometimes begging him "please don't make me do this?!" Knowing full and well that we have to; then get mad at God because we still have to do that thing.

Jesus had spent so much time seeking the will of His Father, trusting the plan and the process to fulfil the plan; that he was obedient to the will of God and not his own free will.

This is why it is so important for us to get into the silent place, into that place of rest with God. So we can hear His voice, so we surrender ourselves to His will.

God had a plan for us before we were born. Isn't that incredible. Could you imagine having a plan for your kiddos before they're even born? Their entire lives planned out and you're trying to lead them and direct them, and they are just not having it. I mean, that's kind of like having two- and three-year-old toddlers, then repeating again as teenagers.

We have their absolute best interest at heart, but they won't stop yelling long enough to even try to understand what we are trying to do for them. They just won't be quiet enough to hear what we have to say.

Every word we say to them, they are ready with a response of some kind for why it's too hard or why they can't possibly, or why they shouldn't have to. Leaving us scratching our heads and wondering how we are going to get through to them.

Do you think God feels the same way with us sometimes? He is trying so desperately to get us to come into that desolate and quiet place to just hear Him out. Listen to what He has to say about things; and there we go ... into that prayer place... ready with a response.

So, how do we stop coming to God, with a response ready, and instead come to him purposing ourselves to get quiet with Him? With a heart open to whatever He wants for us?

Looking back at Luke 5:16 we know that Jesus would withdraw to desolate places ...Do you have a desolate place to get silent with the Lord?

_____

_____

_____

_____

_____

_____

_____

Philippians 4:6-7

"Do not be anxious about anything, but in every situation, by prayer and petition, with thanksgiving, present your requests to God. And the peace of God, which transcends all understanding, will guard your hearts and your minds in Christ Jesus."

We see here there are a few things to keep in mind when entering into the quiet space with God.

First, do not be anxious – God wants us to trust him in every situation.

Second, begin to place your focus on being thankful. Take time to thank him for what you have been given.

Third, present your requests if you have any. You may find after you have spent some time thanking Him for everything you do have that what you went in seeking – or sometimes even begging for, you already have but just did not see it before.

Be still before the Lord and wait patiently for him; fret not yourself over the one who prospers in his way, over the man who carries out evil devices! Psalm 37:7

I want to focus on the first part of this verse. Be still before the Lord and wait patiently for him ... The waiting is what gets most of us off track with our prayer and trust. It goes back to earlier conversation about wanting things right now or done a particular way.

We can also look at Abraham and Sarah's situation again. Sarah struggled to wait on the Lord. I'm sure she was overcome by the voices in her mind reminding her that she was barren, reminding her of her age, telling her this is hopeless, creating so much doubt that she could ever have this baby that was promised.

In this verse we are reminded that finding our peace, strength, and confidence in Him matters. It involves surrendering our worries, fears, and frustrations to Him, knowing that He is our refuge and our source of true rest. It asks us to trust the process regardless of what it looks like.

What are you surrendering to him today? What are you willing to trust Him with as you go through your day, week, month or even this next year?

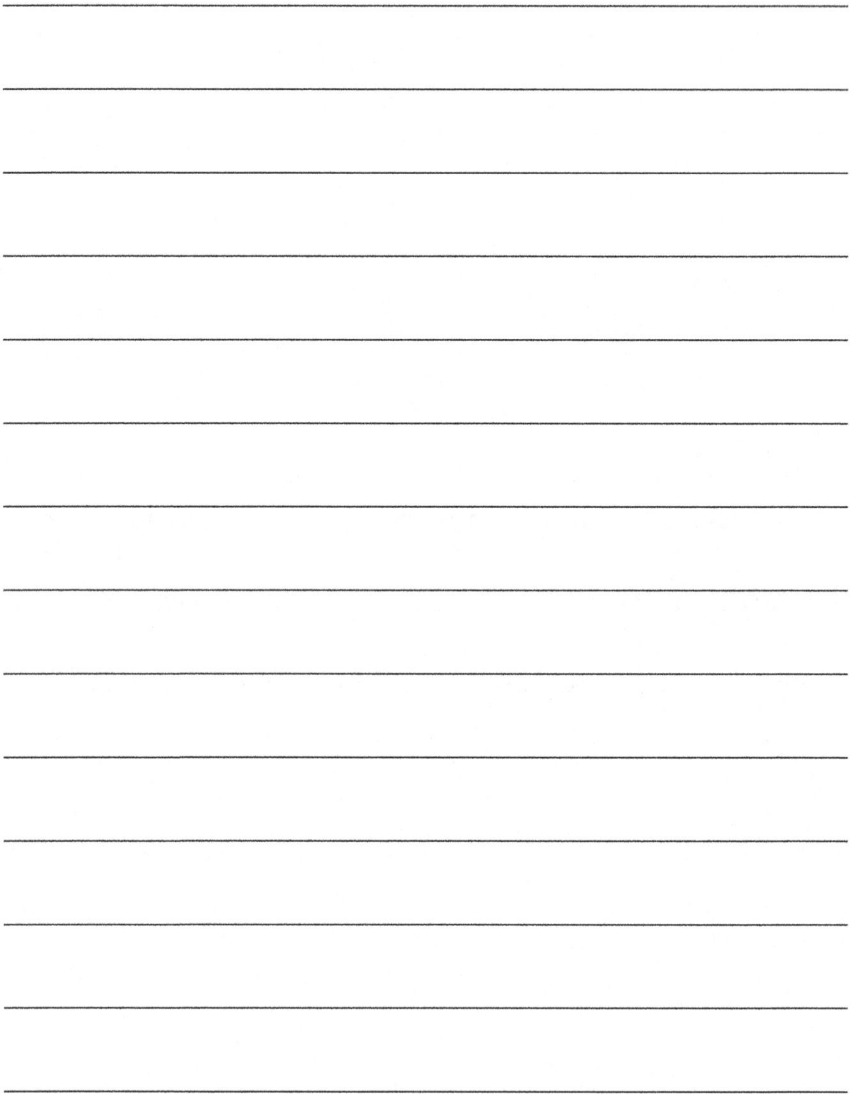

I know that finding things to be thankful for can be hard at times. Especially when there is so much other stuff happening and it seems like this vicious cycle is never going to end.

There are a lot of times when I have wondered,

"Is it ever going to end?"

"Is it ever going to get better?"

"I have been doing the best I can God, when ... "

Too often I feel like we are told to keep looking forward, but sometimes I think it is so important to look back. I think about the man who climbed to the top of Mount Everest.

Do you think he made it all the way to the top without ever looking back to see how far he had climbed? I imagine that sometimes he saw how much more he had to go before reaching the top of that mountain and became very weary. He probably had many thoughts about quitting, just going right back down and being done with it. He probably looked back several times to see how far he had come.

Do you ever take time to look back and see

how far you have come?

What obstacles in life have you overcome already? Trauma? Addiction? Family things? Work things? Sometimes, I think we don't look back enough to see all that God has already brought us through; we don't thank Him enough for it. Instead, we are hyper focused on what is happening right now or on things we are thinking about for the days ahead.

Take a few moments to allow yourself to get into a place of thanksgiving. Write down a few things that you see when you look back on your life ... What has God already brought you through?

_____

_____

_____

_____

_____

_____

_____

_____

You see, God has not left you. He hasn't ever shaken his hands in the air and said, "forget it, I'm done with her!" He has been right there with you all along. Bringing you out of places you never thought could change. Moving people, jobs, medical reports, etc. out of the way so that you, His daughter, could be where you are today.

Now that we have taken some time to thank Him for his goodness and for being such a great Father, we can go in a little deeper.

Take a moment to write down a few things you have been struggling to surrender to the Lord. Things are you are going to take with you into that quiet, desolate place where you can just be silent with Him about for a while.

After you have taken some time to pray for those things you wrote down; don't forget to simply thank Him.

The same God who brought you to where you are today is the same God who already knows your needs and hearts desires.

God doesn't need us to pray over the same things day after day after day; He heard our hearts cry out to him, now we put faith into action and trust Him and the process.

When you feel yourself begin to struggle with the circumstances surrounding you — try to remember to just thank Him.

I find myself thanking Him throughout the day. When my mind begins to wander into those dessert areas, I remember where the living water flows and just begin to thank Him. Thank Him for answering the prayers you haven't even seen the answer to yet. Thank him for where you are. Thank Him for simply being Him – the one who gave His life for ours.

Philippians 4:11 instructs us to be content in all things. This can be tough when the answer we are waiting for doesn't seem like it is ever going to come.

Remembering to keep a thankful heart, looking at what you have, occasionally looking back to see how far you have come, and praise Him through it all because He is a good God. He loves that you have taken time to draw close to him. He loves that you trust Him and have faith to believe that no matter what it looks like, He has a plan. He loves that you want to be involved in His plans and loves even more that you have come to this desolate place seeking that intimate relationship with Him.

You keep him in perfect peace whose mind is stayed on you, because he trusts in you. Isaiah 26:3

Those silent moments with God will make His ways, His plans, His answers easier to understand and even accept.

Remember, growth happens in silence.

Made in the USA
Monee, IL
23 October 2023